J.D. HILL

Rideshare Driver Hacks That Work

Your Quick & Easy Guide to More Money and Higher Ratings

This book was professionally typeset on Reedsy.
Find out more at reedsy.com

Contents

Disclaimers   1

Introduction   3

Hack 1: It's Not Always About You   6

Hack 2: This Is A Business   8

Hack 3: Keep It Moving   10

Hack 4: Decide How Much Your Time Is Worth...And
Stick To It   12

Hack 5: Communicate, Communicate, Communicate   14

Make a Difference with Your Review!   17

Hack 6: Accept Riders As They Are Unless There Is A Safety...   21

Hack 7: Create Rapport or Get Reported   23

Hack 8: Declare Your Independence   27

Hack 9: Go Offline When Necessary   29

Bonus: Food Delivery Hacks   31

Hack 1: Fast Food Restaurants   32

Hack 2: Your No-Go List   33

Hack 3: The Best Place To Put The Delivery For No-Contact...   34

Hack 4: A Simple Way To Save Time For In-Person Deliveries   35

Keeping the Game Alive   36

Conclusion   38

Disclaimers

1. This book is based on my own experiences and learning on the road as a driver for major rideshare platforms. I hope that when you apply these Hacks to your own work, you will have similar or even better results! However, individual results may vary. There are many variables that could impact your success or lack thereof, such as your level of effort in reading and applying the Hacks, the time you spend on the road doing the work, platform policies/Community Guidelines changing, changes in the law in your area, changes in your market conditions like the supply of drivers and demand of riders, weather/climate, your skill level, and other factors. Therefore, I cannot guarantee any specific results. I can only share my own experience and knowledge and hope that these Hacks are helpful to you as well in earning more money and higher ratings.

2 .The ideas and opinions in this book are my own, and they may be different from yours. However, you most likely bought it in order to learn something new, find solutions to problems, and/or open yourself up to a different perspective. If you disagree with something, please consider applying it and seeing if it creates a positive change. If you ever feel offended by something I have written or feel that it is too strongly worded, please know that that is not my intent. I am trying to help you, and based on what I have observed and read by and about other drivers,

there are some helpful things that I feel need to be written, which is why I have included them.

3. I have written this book to assist drivers working in the United States in the 2020s, yet have designed these Hacks to be as timeless and location-independent as possible. Still, if you drive in Canada or some other country now or in the future, not all of the information may apply to you and your specific situation. Please learn from it what you can and disregard the rest.

Introduction

You now have what I hope will be the last guide to rideshare driving that you'll ever need - Rideshare Driver Hacks That Work: Your Quick & Easy Guide to More Money and Higher Ratings! What you are about to read came from my experience of giving several thousand rides in the past two years.

This book would be helpful and hopefully game-changing for any rideshare driver, but I have geared it mostly to those who are signed up and are comfortable with using the driver app(s). If you haven't yet signed up as a driver or are still learning the basics, you may want to review other resources and tools first and then come back to this when you're ready.

What is it about being a driver now that makes it not only possible, but necessary to work smarter if you want to earn the most money and highest ratings? Recently, rideshare driving changed almost overnight when one platform and then another allowed us to see the time, distance, fare, and approximate pickup and drop-off locations of each ride. Somehow, though, in revealing this information, it was also possible at times for the platforms to lower the amount of money we were paid. If you want to earn as much or more than you were paid before, you need to adapt, and that means making changes first in your mind and then in the way you play the rideshare game.

This means acting in your own best interest and in the interest of your riders by using your time, money, and fuel as efficiently as possible. My goal is not to waste your time or beat around the bush. It is to be clear, direct, and honest so that you can get the message, pick up your phone, turn on your vehicle, and be more successful with earnings and ratings than you ever thought possible!

This book will not discuss which phone mount or dashcam to use, which rideshare insurance to purchase, or which vehicle or platform is best. That information changes as markets and technologies evolve. The focus will be on what YOU can control – YOUR mindset, how YOU operate YOUR business to earn as much money as YOU can, and how YOU drive and interact with YOUR riders to improve YOUR ratings.

We'll cover topics that when you first read them may seem obvious. They're included because they're so fundamental to your success that they bear repeating and focusing on. On its face, driving people around from place to place with GPS directions may not be a difficult task for you, but to perform significantly better than others in earnings and ratings, it helps to focus on the fundamentals and maintain a winning mindset. Trust me – you have in your hands what you'll need to take your rideshare business to the next level, so bear with me on this!

The value of higher earnings is obvious. But why focus on higher ratings? First, you may be eligible for perks if you reach or exceed a certain level. There are also some intangibles, like taking pride in a job very well done, riders' perceptions that they will be able to enjoy an especially good ride with you, and the higher likelihood that you will receive a tip for earning yet another perfect "5". However, probably the best reason to focus on keeping your rating as high as possible and delivering the quality behind it on ride after ride is to minimize your chances of being reported to the rideshare companies by riders for various issues. You'll see more on this topic in Hack .7

A final note - many of these ideas, sayings, and words of what I hope you will find to be wisdom were things that I came up with and repeated to myself over and over again in the car – to stay on task and continue earning no matter the day, night, or season. I routinely earn between $40-50 per hour as a rideshare driver in the Upstate New York region and currently have ratings of 4.97 and 5.00 on the two platforms. Depending on the season, I drive between 20-40 hours each week.

But enough about me. This is about you, so let's get to it!

Hack 1: It's Not Always About You

Is being a rideshare driver really "about" you? Like many things in life, it depends. Sometimes it is about you, and sometimes it isn't. Let's begin with when it isn't.

Outside your vehicle, it's not about you. Why is this important? Because inside your vehicle, it IS about you, and therefore you CAN influence – and often control – what goes on there. You SHOULD NOT EXPECT YOURSELF ever to influence what goes on outside the vehicle, especially as it relates to how the platforms do business. We apply to be independent contractors, and if approved, 1. they give us access to their network of riders as well as policies and Community Guidelines to follow, 2. we give rides, and 3. we get paid. It's that simple.

This means:

1. You are not entitled to receive a particular amount of money for your work BUT if you work smarter, you can earn far more than drivers working for other companies who are paid by the hour as employees.

2. You are not entitled to benefits that employees sometimes receive BUT you can receive benefits that most employees can only dream of

like flexible hours, unlimited access to work, in-state travel opportunities, and extended vacations.

3. You are responsible for paying your own expenses BUT you have access to tax write-offs that can reduce your taxable income and qualify you for programs such as subsidized health insurance usually available only to people who earn less than you.

4. Whether you receive a ride and how busy it is has nothing to do with your inherent value as a person BUT when you do receive a ride, you can make your rider's day and earn tips based on who YOU are as a person and how effectively you perform the work.

5. They offer what they offer at a particular time in a particular place. You can either accept or reject any ride request BUT you can know your market well enough to be able to predict where to go and when to go there so you'll be more likely to receive a greater number of offers to choose from.

Hack 2: This Is A Business

Obvious statement alert – of course this is a business! I highly doubt that any of us are doing this to raise money for charity. We're out there at all hours of the day and night in all kinds of weather because we've got bills to pay, things to save up for, kids to support, and dreams to turn into reality.

Here's why this is so important to remember anytime you're online looking for a ride or driving people around: **every moment that you are in your vehicle is an opportunity to earn money.** You'll spend the same amount of time online if you a) sit in the vehicle waiting for a ride, or b) based on where you see in the driver app that the other drivers are, drive around trying to find a less busy location. The same goes for a) sitting outside the pickup destination waiting for the rider to get in, vs. b) getting out of the vehicle to call the rider's name or driving closer to the rider to get them into the vehicle faster so you can begin the ride sooner. Also consider that you are running a business when you decide between spending some of the time you scheduled yourself to drive with a) fixing a low-priority, low dollar-figure problem with a platform's support team, or b) going out, getting another ride, and making the same or even greater amount in far less time.

Every strategy you'll ever learn to be more efficient or more effective comes from this fact - you are, indeed, running a business! This applies whether this is your full-time, only gig or if it is a side hustle. Your goal is to make the most out of every minute and mile, avoiding distractions or anything else that would keep you from earning money and higher ratings!

Hack 3: Keep It Moving

As a rideshare driver, you get paid the most when your vehicle is in motion. Avoid sitting in airport queues or waiting around anywhere for rides for more than a few minutes. It's possible to look at the rider app for the platform you're using to see where the closest six or seven other drivers are. If you see that there are lots of other drivers around you, then you're not needed in that place at that time. It's nothing personal, it's just the reality. Plus, remember - that is outside your vehicle, so it's not about you! Instead, look for another place nearby where there aren't other drivers and where there might actually be a need at that time - a shopping center, a big box store, a college, a large event, the entertainment district where bars and clubs are, or a lower-income area where there might be more people who need rides because they don't have their own vehicles. As you get more practice at this in your market and keep refining your strategy, you'll figure out where and when the hot spots and times are likely to be. Then, YOU'LL be the closest driver and will get the offers that those other drivers still waiting around in a cluster of vehicles will never get. A herd mentality simply does not work in this business.

Remember - part of being an independent contractor is taking advantage of tax benefits like deductions for mileage, insurance, and phone plans. It is definitely worth exploring such options by consulting with a tax professional. If you find that the mileage deduction is advantageous to your situation, for example, then staying in motion will help you earn a greater tax write-off.

This is simple, but bears repeating - get the rider in your vehicle ASAP! Once you drop off your current rider and before you head to your next pick-up, message that next rider that you are on your way. At the same time, send a second message: "Please be ready. Thanks" or something like that if you prefer to say it in another polite way. Then, when you arrive, message them again that you are at the pick-up spot.

This should be a win-win - you are letting them know that you plan to get them to their destination ASAP, and you are using your time as efficiently as possible. They may cancel the ride while you are en route if they can't be ready by the time you arrive, but this is actually positive. Then, you will not be wasting your time waiting for them and can be available to pick up another rider!

You can choose how long you are willing to wait for your rider to get into your vehicle once you arrive. This will depend on how busy it is at that time with ride requests and therefore how likely it is that you will quickly receive another ride request. (Plus, while you're waiting, if necessary, you can turn the car around so that it's already in the direction you'll be going on your route.) Just be sure not to wait so long that doing so works against you.

Hack 4: Decide How Much Your Time Is Worth...And Stick To It

I t could be $30, $40, or even more per hour. Whatever you decide is totally up to you. In reality, either the market will bear it or it won't. Test the market at that time and see how much you can earn when the base fare, bonuses, and tips are factored in.

Let's say that you want to earn $30 per hour. This could be in the form of one $30 ride that lasts one hour, two 30-minute rides that pay $15, or even six 10-minute rides that pay $5. It will most likely never work out exactly in this way, but if you review every request with the intention to have the amount it pays meet your hourly rate in proportion to the length of time that it will take, then over several hours or days, you will most likely earn at least your hourly rate on average!

To know the true value of a ride, though, the trick is to include the amount of time that it will take for you to get back to a place where you will be likely to pick up another rider. This is why, in my opinion, you should avoid the possibility of "backtracking" (driving back to where you started without another rider) whenever possible. Let's take the example of a 30-minute ride that pays $15. On the surface, that ride would meet your $30 per hour rate. However, it would only TRULY meet that rate if you were likely to pick up another rider at the end of the first 30-minute ride that would also meet your $30 rate. If you drive 30 minutes away from a busy area and are in the middle of nowhere at the end of it, then it's likely that you would spend the next 30 minutes driving back to where you started WITHOUT another rider. That would render your hour worth only $15 - half of your desired rate.

Ride requests come in fast, and maybe you are in a market that you're not very familiar with yet and can't discern quickly enough whether the destination is in a remote or busy area. However, with experience and practice, you will know where the busier areas are and when they are likely to be the busiest. Obviously, in general, cities are busier than suburban towns, and those towns are busier than rural areas.

Finally - STICK TO IT!! This requires some discipline, of course, but success in this or any gig economy business is about learning fundamentals - even as simple as this - and repeating them over and over again. Nothing is ever exact, and yes, there might be that one "unicorn" of a ride that you'll get in the middle of the night on a quiet country road, but DO NOT count on this. Instead, focus on and follow this fundamental practice, and you will see the benefits in the amounts you're able to earn over time.

Hack 5: Communicate, Communicate, Communicate

This bears repeating - as soon as you are on your way to pick up a rider, use the driver app to message the rider to tell them that. One platform has the message option to say that you'll arrive in ____ minutes, while the other simply lets you tell the rider "I'm on my way". Also message the rider "Please be ready. Thanks." or some other polite version of this if you'd prefer. In my experience, doing this has greatly improved the likelihood that the rider will be ready for me when I arrive. When you do arrive, message them again to let them know that you're there.

If you are going to an especially busy area like an entertainment district or a busy college campus where there will likely be a crowd of people, call the rider while you are on the way and arrange to meet them in a certain place. This is especially useful in situations like the bar closing time when the area is very crowded and there are lots of other drivers looking for their riders. Consider keeping them on the line while you are trying to find each other so that doing so is that much easier.

Most of the time, when you arrive, it will be clear where they are. However, if you're picking them up in a place where there are lots of people around and you still can't find them, "communication" can take a different form. First, in the driver app, find their approximate location relative to where you are, drive the vehicle as close to them as you safely and legally can, lower your window, and call their name. This will often work. If it doesn't, then get out of the vehicle and look for them. One platform shows their photo and the other doesn't, but regardless, call their name out in as loud a voice as you can. Quite often, they'll hear you, follow you back to the vehicle, and thank you for doing this for them! Social customs be damned, you are running a business, time is money, and you need them in your vehicle ASAP so you can get them where they need to go ASAP so you can get to your next rider ASAP!

Whenever you can, **THANK THEM.** If they are ready for you when you arrive, thank them for their promptness. At the end of the ride, thank them for their business. This is a service industry role, and they likely had other options for getting where they wanted to go, so whenever you can, showing gratitude - and the humility to give it - is a winning move. This might be the only service that your rider can afford or access, so it will likely make them feel good to be cared for and appreciated in just this small, simple way. They may also be more likely to tip you!

Some other times when communication can help:

1. If a rider appears to be sick, tell them that if you need them to pull over, then they can tell you and you'll do that. If they ask you to do this, then pull over in a safe place ASAP so they can open the door or simply take a break if needed. Simply doing this has saved me many times from having a rider vomit in my car.

2. If you are ever doing something non-standard for any reason – like turning the car around or pulling over, for example – tell the rider that

you're doing this and why. Maybe you're turning the car around on a dead end street so you can go back in the direction of your route or you're pulling over to let an aggressive driver behind you pass. The purpose of communicating with the rider in situations like this is to help them feel comfortable if you're about to do something they're not expecting.

3. If the rider has a cup with them, let them know where the cupholder is. This can help avoid spills in your vehicle.

4. If a rider appears to be in a hurry to catch a plane or get somewhere else on time, ask them "How are we doing on time for you?" They'll tell you, and if they truly are in a hurry, you can assure them that you'll do your best to get them there ASAP and they'll know that you're on their side. Then, get them to their destination ASAP safely and without violating laws or Community Guidelines.

Make a Difference with Your Review!

Unlock the Power of Generosity

"Money can't buy happiness, but giving it away can." - Freddie Mercury

Hey there, amazing reader! Did you know that people who give without expecting anything in return tend to have happier and more fulfilling lives? And guess what? They often end up making more money too! So, let's grab this chance to spread some joy and kindness together.

I've got a super important favor to ask you...

Would you be willing to help out someone you've never met, even if you don't get a shoutout for it?

Who's this mystery person, you ask? Well, they're a lot like you. Maybe a bit less experienced, eager to make a difference in the world of rideshare, and looking for that golden nugget of wisdom. They need guidance but don't know where to find it.

My big goal is to share the coolest rideshare driving Hacks with everyone. Everything I do is all about that mission. But to really make it happen, I need to reach... well, everyone!

And here's where you, my awesome reader, come into play. Most folks do judge a book by its cover (and its reviews). So, here's a little request from me for a driver out there who could really use your help:

Could you please take a moment to leave a review for this book?

This little act of kindness won't cost you a dime and takes less than a minute, but it could totally change another driver's life. Your review might just be the push they need to...

...help another local business thrive in their community.

...support them as an entrepreneur in making their family's dreams come true.

...transform their lives for the better.

...make another dream a reality.

AND...ensure countless riders reach their destinations safely and happily.

To get that warm, fuzzy feeling and make a real difference, all you need to do is...

drop a quick review.

Just scan the QR code right here to leave your thoughts:

[https://www.amazon.com/review/review-your-purchases/?asin=B
0CR8CJW44]

If the idea of helping a fellow driver brings a smile to your face, then
you're definitely my kind of person. Welcome to the club! You're now
part of our cool gang.

I can't wait to help you boost your earnings and ratings beyond what
you thought possible. You're gonna love the Hacks I've got lined up for
you in the next chapters.

A huge thank you from the deepest part of my heart. Now, let's dive
back into our awesome journey.

- Your biggest cheerleader, J.D. Hill

P.S. - Fun fact: When you offer something valuable to someone else, you become more valuable to them. If you think this book is a gem for another driver, why not share it with them? Spread the love!

Hack 6: Accept Riders As They Are Unless There Is A Safety Issue

Anyone could need a ride. Your riders are from all walks of life and are diverse in every way imaginable. Therefore, it's likely that you come in contact with those from different cultures, who have different political views, and who have different lifestyles. This understanding is built into the platforms' Community Guidelines, but on a ride-by-ride basis, this just comes down to simple acceptance.

Let them have their opinions if they want to share them, listen to their views whether you agree or disagree, and don't try to convince them that your view is the right one. Let them have their fun or their silence or their phone call or their music or their noise. Let them put down the window or ask you to adjust the temperature in the vehicle. You're running a business and they're letting you have their dollars, so when it's safe to do so, let them be as they are. Most of the time, it will only make a positive difference. You're just giving them a ride, and you'll probably never see them again after it's over. If they feel accepted, they'll also feel more comfortable and more likely to tip you and give you a higher rating.

Of course, there is a limit to this. There are some things that they should not be allowed to do, like smoke or damage your vehicle. And yes, there are some times when their words or actions truly do make a difference.. If they're threatening, violent, or make you feel unsafe, the platforms have guidelines for dealing with this. For example, I've had someone make sexual advances to me, so I reported them.

In the end, if you treat people with respect, most people will respect you too. Unfortunately, some people are disrespectful no matter how they're treated. They might just be having a bad day or they might behave like that all the time. You'll probably never know. However, their dollars are just as green as anyone else's, so worst-case scenario, just finish the ride and rate them low enough so you're not paired with them again.

How can you avoid or at least reduce the likelihood of uncomfortable situations in your vehicle? The next Hack is designed to help you with just that.

Hack 7: Create Rapport or Get Reported

The reality is that the rideshare platforms set up your independent contractor relationship with them in ways that are advantageous to them. One of their advantages is that they can suspend or even deactivate your driver account for things about you, your car, or your driving that riders report to them, whether those reports are true or not. Unless you have a dashcam - which I highly recommend getting - that can prove your innocence and the rider's dishonesty, it's just your word against the rider's, and the rideshare company may side with the rider since that's the person paying for the service.

This is the sad but true situation that we as rideshare drivers find ourselves in. I have read several posts in social media groups by drivers with stories of being deactivated after having been falsely accused of misconduct by the rider just because the driver enforced a policy, said "no" to the rider's request, or upset the rider in some way. In my experience of several thousand successful rides, though, this can all be avoided by creating rapport with the rider and always remembering this simple saying: **Create rapport or get reported.**

Here's how to create and maintain rapport as best you can:

Remember the Big Picture

This is rideshare, not delivery. You are driving around people with unique identities, thoughts, feelings, personalities, opinions, and stories. Many of them may not have anyone in their lives willing to listen to them or understand them, and in our modern society, many of them will be suffering in one way or another.

Giving a ride to someone you've never met presents a challenge and an opportunity. You know very little about your rider, so it can be challenging to find something in common or that you can relate to about each other. However, their ride with you may be the one time in their day that they can take a break if they want to, let go of their identity, and gain a fresh outlook on life by being with you, a friendly stranger who won't judge them. Playing that role is your golden opportunity to deliver great service, get a 5-star rating, and even earn a tip.

Relate to your rider

We are all human. Still, you may have much in common with your rider or very little. If they're willing to engage, then try to find topics or experiences that you have in common with them. Sometimes this will be obvious and sometimes it won't. It can help to simply ask them how their day is going and go from there. If nothing is apparent, there's the old favorite - the weather and how we like it to be.

Be Humble

We have so many advantages as rideshare drivers compared to people working as standard employees, but another reality - no matter how we feel about it - is that we are replaceable. There is no getting around that fact. It takes some level of skill and experience to be able to run your business as efficiently as possible and maximize your earnings as a driver, but the simple task of driving riders from one place to another only takes the ability to drive. If a less experienced rideshare driver earns far less than you do per hour, then that's an opportunity for the driver to improve, but the rider still reached the destination and it's likely that the rideshare company still earned the same amount of money it would have had you been the driver instead.

Yes, it's your vehicle, but you are providing a service to your rider and welcoming them as a guest. You'll earn far more money in the long run in tips and additional rides by being humble, providing outstanding service, and allowing them to customize their experience in your vehicle within reason and the bounds of laws and Community Guidelines. For example, you would not want to allow them to damage your vehicle or make a mess, but they should be able to adjust the windows, music, and temperature to their liking and with your assistance if needed.

Take a Break

If for whatever reason you've reached your limit, you're tired, hungry, thirsty, out of patience, or frustrated, then simply take a break. This is using one of the advantages that we have of being our own boss - signing on or off the driver app whenever we'd like instead of following a set schedule. Just as flight attendants advise us to make sure we have oxygen before helping another person put on an oxygen mask in the event of an emergency, we have to take care of ourselves before we can take care of our riders. You don't want to take "just one more ride" and then have that rider be the one who is difficult and requires a lot of patience.

Say "Yes" When You Can

The lifetime value of having access to a rideshare driver app can be immense and in the tens or even hundreds of thousands of dollars. It's simply not worth risking the loss of your access because of one "bad" ride. Therefore, if a rider makes a request that you can say "yes" to because it doesn't violate laws or Community Guidelines — like turning the music up or down, listening to a certain radio station, putting the window down, turning up the heat, getting a charge for their smartphone, or taking an alternate route — then say "yes" to it.

Let It Go

If you're having a "bad" ride, then do what you need to do to get through it - except something that will make it worse - and then let it go. During the ride, sometimes being silent and taking deep breaths can help. Maybe changing the topic of conversation or putting on some calm music will change the energy in your vehicle. Remind yourself that the ride will last just ____ more minutes and that you can rate the rider appropriately at the end. If you say anything more, just be sure to watch your tone so it's not sarcastic or condescending.

Once the ride is over and you've congratulated yourself for getting through it, check in with yourself to see if you're hungry, tired, or thirsty. Then, act accordingly and consider following the tip above and taking a break if you'd like. You're within your rights to do that!

Hack 8: Declare Your Independence

We're independent contractors, but this isn't just an employment status - it's the basis of how you run your business. Our nation declared its independence from a colonizer, and as a rideshare driver, you have declared your independence from traditional employment, with its set hours, set pay rate, and regular supervision. In exchange for paying our own taxes and expenses, we have the freedom to work when, where, and mostly how we want as long as we follow laws and a platform's Community Guidelines. However, your own declaration of independence doesn't have to end at the sign-up stage. Instead, boldly declare your independence through how you operate your business, how you drive, and how you treat your riders. Here's how:

1. Use GPS as a tool - GPS is your friend, not your boss or your jailor. It is a tool that is always there to help. When you're in an unfamiliar city, it's probably your best friend!. However, if you're familiar with where you are and know a faster way to get somewhere to avoid traffic, accidents, or too many traffic lights, make the *independent* decision to take that alternate route. Also, if a rider wants to go a different way and you know it'll get you there, then again in the spirit of saying "yes" when you can, go that way.

2. Avoid traffic lights and traffic whenever possible - If you have the option of taking the highway, take it. If you can take a side street that helps you avoid a traffic light, use it. If it's safe and legal to do so, make a 3-point turn or pull into and out of a driveway instead of driving around the block. Depending on the distance of the ride and the layout of roads, simply doing this can shave 15% of more of the distance and several minutes off of your ride.

3. Drive in places where and at times when there are fewer drivers and/or more riders. As long as you feel safe, this can be a great way to earn money, especially when other places are busy. Drive in potentially difficult weather conditions if it's safe to do so. Drive at night. Pick up riders from clubs and bars.

4. Be yourself as long as your riders appreciate it - There are no uniforms or office politics involved in rideshare. Wear what you'd like, play your favorite music, discuss your interests if you'd like, and relate to your riders as yourself. As with other places, though, try to avoid discussions of politics, religion, or sports teams unless the rider brings up these topics and you can comment on them in a way that will build rapport.

Hack 9: Go Offline When Necessary

Working as a rideshare driver has changed a great deal in such a short time. All of the Hacks you've learned so far are set up to help you succeed at times and in markets where others may fail. They're set up to keep you operating at peak levels and to earn as much money and the highest average rating possible. However, if there are too many drivers, lower fares, and lower ridership, there may come a time when you're using your Hacks, you're in an awesome mood, and you're set up for success, but you're still not earning the money that you want or need. At times like these - for fifteen minutes or forever - you can make the ultimate move: going offline.

First, what can you do when you are often driving around looking for riders and it's not working?

1. Go offline temporarily - maybe for 15 minutes or an hour - until you see it getting busier.

2. Turn on other options in the rideshare apps you already use. For example, maybe food delivery is busier or turning on the ability to give rides to people with pets would help.

3. Prepare for times like these by signing up for other apps for tasks

such as food delivery or grocery shopping so you have your access to them in your back pocket if you ever need them. Then, you can give yourself more ways to earn money when the time comes. To maximize your chances of success, try to stay current with which gig economy apps are available in your market so you can sign up for any new ones that you're interested in and that you qualify for.

4. Drive rideshare at different times and maybe even in a different market nearby to see if the situation is any different. You can even turn on destination mode in the rideshare platform and pick up a rider for the trip to or from the other market if the stars align and you get lucky.

If this isn't possible for your situation or if you've tried and it hasn't worked, then it may be time to go offline for good. You can always try again in the next week, month, or year to see if things have gotten better, but if they haven't, it won't be for lack of trying!

Bonus: Food Delivery Hacks

Hack 1: Fast Food Restaurants

A lways go inside fast food restaurants to pick up your orders there. Especially since the pandemic, most customers wait in the drive-thru, and most restaurants don't yet have separate lanes for delivery driver pick-ups. This simple Hack can save you lots of time because it will often enable you to skip ahead to the front of the line or close to it.

If you can't go inside a fast food restaurant once the dining room closes in the evening, don't pick up any orders at that restaurant. Otherwise, you'll likely be waiting in the drive-thru along with the other customers and delivery drivers. Waiting there is simply not an efficient use of your time.

Hack 2: Your No-Go List

I f and when you ever pick up an order from a restaurant that for whatever reason doesn't get it to you as soon as you arrive or pretty close to it, add this restaurant to your no-go list. Complete the delivery and then don't accept orders from the restaurant again until after 2-3 months, when you might consider giving them another chance to see if they've improved their operations.

Delays could be due to understaffing, poor management, inexperienced staff, or the fact that they're very busy, but this should not be your problem. Your goal is to accept orders that are worth your time and then pick them up and deliver them. It's just that simple. Well-run privately-owned and not chain restaurants are often your best bets, but you'll discover which ones to work with in your market. Just don't waste your time waiting for excessive amounts of time or dealing with other inefficiencies that make it more difficult to meet your income goals as a delivery driver.

Hack 3: The Best Place To Put The Delivery For No-Contact Orders

This is an easy one and may be common sense, but maybe not. Of course, you'll always follow the customer's general directions on where to leave the order, such as by the front or back door. When you get to that place, though, place the order in such a way that when the customer opens the door, the bag and any other items won't fall or be knocked down and will also be within arm's reach. Often, this will be on the other side of the door so that when that door swings open, the customer will be able to easily pick up the items without having to exit where they are. Simply look at the door and its hinges, figure out the direction in which it opens, and make sure that you're not putting the order in its path. Otherwise, the customer might have to put on their shoes, gingerly open the door a crack, and then carefully pick up the order before bringing it back inside. This might not make a difference to all of your customers, but especially when it's raining, snowing, or especially hot or cold and they don't want to have to go outside, this simple attention to detail could make a big difference to them.

Hack 4: A Simple Way To Save Time For In-Person Deliveries

L et's say that you've picked up the food order, you're back in your vehicle about to drive to the customer, and the delivery app shows you that it'll take five minutes to get there to deliver the order to the customer in person. Immediately call the customer and let them know that you'll be there in five minutes and that you'll see them then. This Hack is a win-win. They'll get their food sooner, and it will be much more likely that they'll be ready to meet you as soon as you arrive. This way, you won't have to wait for them to come to you and you can move on to your next pick-up that much sooner.

Keeping the Game Alive

Congratulations on finishing the book! Now that you've got the tools to earn more and get those top ratings, it's time to spread the word.

By leaving your honest opinion about this book on Amazon, you're not just sharing your thoughts – you're guiding other drivers to the information they've been searching for. You're passing the torch of rideshare wisdom.

Thank you for being a part of this journey. The Hacks stay alive and thrive when we share our knowledge. By leaving your review, you're doing just that.

Ready to share your thoughts? Click here to leave your review on Amazon.

[https://www.amazon.com/review/review-your-purchases/?asin
=B0CR8CJW44]

Your review means the world to me and to every rideshare driver out
there searching for guidance. Thanks for keeping the game alive!

Conclusion

And there you have them - rideshare and some bonus delivery Hacks that work for earning more money and higher ratings. I hope that they help you succeed no matter where or when you apply them.

One final word, though - innovate! With how quickly rideshare changes, you may very well discover Hacks of your own. There will always be new and better ways of doing things, and there will undoubtedly be new products, services, and other changes in policies or earnings structures that the rideshare platforms throw at us. With that in mind:

1. Try something new to see if it makes a difference. For example, is there a different way that you could say or do something that would make things with a rider or ride go better next time?

2. If you receive a less than perfect rating, is there something you did or didn't do that caused that? It could have been the rider's fault, but maybe not. Consider changing your approach to see if that helps.

3. Did you deviate from an approach that was working? If so, why? Did it help?

4. Did you make a mistake? If you did, then OK, it was most likely just a learning experience. You're aware of it now and far less likely to make the same mistake again.

Hit the road, enjoy your rides, and be safe out there!